HOUSE
IT GOING?

A FUN AND PRACTICAL
GUIDE TO HOMEBUYING

ANGELA PINAMONTI

HOUSE IT GOING?

A Fun And Practical Guide To Homebuying

Copyright © 2025 by Angela Pinamonti

CONTENTS

DEDICATION

This book is dedicated to all aspiring homeowners, current homeowners, and real estate investors—the brave souls who dream of financial independence and the sweet, sweet security of owning a home, preferably one without mysterious plumbing noises or a looming landlord.

It's a testament to the power of diligent planning, smart saving (and let's be honest, a little bit of luck), and a disciplined approach to personal finance that doesn't involve hiding money in a mattress.

This work is for those willing to put in the effort to build a secure future for themselves and their families—a future that hopefully involves fewer arguments about whose turn it is to mow the lawn and more debates about what shade of "greige" to paint the ridiculously expensive, yet totally worth it, new kitchen cabinets.

It is dedicated to everyone who believes in the transformative power of homeownership: a place to build memories, cultivate stability, and secure a legacy for generations to come.

To those who see their home not merely as shelter, but as a cornerstone of their financial well-being and a symbol of their hard work and aspirations—this book is for you.

It is a tribute to the tenacity and vision of countless individuals who have worked tirelessly to achieve their homeownership goals—proving that with determination, a solid financial plan, and maybe a slightly more flexible definition of "spacious," the dream of owning a home is attainable for everyone who commits to the journey.

We hope this book provides you with the tools and knowledge to confidently navigate the path to homeownership—and maybe even a few laughs along the way. Because let's face it, buying a house is hilarious (in a slightly terrifying, stress-induced kind of way).

FOREWORD

The dream of homeownership: a picket fence, a golden retriever slobbering on the welcome mat, and maybe, *just maybe*, enough leftover money for avocado toast once a month.

For generations, owning a home has been a defining milestone, symbolizing stability, security, and a critical step in building long-term wealth. But let's be honest—the process of buying a home is anything but simple.

Between saving for a down payment, figuring out what on earth "escrow" actually means, and surviving the soul-crushing process of making an offer (only to be outbid by an all-cash buyer who probably owns a private island), the road to homeownership can feel overwhelming.

That's why this book exists—to guide you through the madness of buying a home, helping you make smart financial decisions along the way.

Whether you're:

- ✓ A first-time homebuyer (*brave soul!*),
- ✓ An aspiring investor (*even braver!*), or
- ✓ A current homeowner wondering if selling is worth the hassle,

this book will walk you through every step of the process in a way that's clear, practical, and, most importantly—**not boring**.

So buckle up, grab a calculator (*and maybe a stress ball*), and let's navigate the wild world of homeownership together.

INTRODUCTION

Welcome to homebuying, where dreams are made, budgets are tested, and "fixer-upper" can mean anything from "just needs paint" to "should be condemned."

Buying a home isn't just about scrolling Zillow until you find something cute. It's about building a financial foundation that allows you to make informed, confident decisions—instead of panic-Googling "how much house can I afford" at 2 a.m.

That's where this book comes in.

"House it Going? A Fun and Practical Guide to Homebuying" is your essential roadmap to navigating the complex, *sometimes absurd*, but ultimately rewarding world of real estate.

What You'll Learn in This Book:

✓ **How to get your finances in order** so you're *actually* ready to buy
✓ **How to budget realistically** (*because it's not just about the mortgage payment!*)
✓ **How to understand mortgages, closing costs, and contracts** without falling asleep
✓ **How to spot red flags when house hunting** (*because nobody wants a surprise termite infestation*)

✓ **How to handle inspections, negotiations, and escrow** without losing your mind
✓ **How to keep your home from turning into a money pit** (*yes, maintenance is a thing!*)
✓ **How to buy a second property as an investment** (*without selling a kidney*)

What Makes This Book Different?

This is not your typical dry, financial how-to book that makes you feel like you need a degree in economics to understand it.

This book keeps it real. It's written for people who want practical advice, explained in normal language (not mortgage-speak), with a dash of humor to keep things entertaining.

Who Is This Book For?

▸ First-time buyers who want to avoid rookie mistakes (*and still have money left for furniture*).
▸ Homeowners thinking about selling and upgrading (or downsizing).
▸ Aspiring real estate investors looking to make smart moves.
▸ Anyone who wants to feel confident about their homebuying decisions—without the stress migraines.

Why? Because homeownership isn't just about buying a house. It's about building a secure financial future.

So grab a coffee (or margarita, we won't judge), and let's turn your dream of homeownership into a reality.

This book is designed to be your go-to guide—whether you're just getting started, in the middle of the process, or wondering how the heck you're going to maintain this thing once you own it. So let's dive in. Because whether you're buying, selling, or investing—the best thing you can do is be prepared. And remember: if real estate were easy, everyone would own beachfront property. By the time you finish this book, you'll not only understand the homebuying process, but you'll also be confident, financially prepared, and ready to handle whatever homeownership throws your way.

(Yes, even the mysterious plumbing noises.)

Let's get started!

CHAPTER 1

Are You Financially Ready to Commit?

(Or Are You Just Flirting with the Idea?)

Buying a home is a lot like dating. At first, it's all excitement and possibility—you swipe through listings late at night, imagining a future with each one. Then, you find "the one." You picture your life there: sipping coffee in the kitchen, hosting friends in the backyard, maybe even adopting a dog to match the aesthetic. It's perfect. You're in love.

But before you go picking out backsplash tiles and Googling "how to DIY shiplap," let's have the talk. No, not the "where is this relationship going?" talk. The "are you financially ready to buy a home?" talk. Because, just like a relationship, homeownership is all fun and games until the bills start rolling in.

So, are you ready to take the plunge, or are you just flirting with the idea of homeownership? **Let's find out.**

1. The Ultimate Reality Check: Can You Actually Afford This?

If buying a home were just about making a monthly mortgage payment, life would be easy. But, like a first date that goes surprisingly well, there are hidden surprises you didn't see coming—property taxes, maintenance, insurance, and the occasional unexpected "oops" that drains your bank account faster than you can say "homeownership."

Here's a quick checklist to see if you're truly ready:

- ☐ You have stable income. (Freelancers, take a deep breath.)
- ☐ You have savings for a down payment.
- ☐ You have additional savings for closing costs (yep, that's extra).
- ☐ Your credit score isn't a dumpster fire.
- ☐ You're ready to commit to one location for at least a few years.
- ☐ You can handle unexpected expenses without selling a kidney.

If you checked all those boxes, congratulations! You're possibly ready.

If not, no shame—this chapter is here to help.

2. The Terrifying Yet Essential Credit Score Talk

(aka: Please Stop Ignoring Your Credit Score)

Your credit score is basically your financial dating profile. It tells lenders how responsible you are with money and whether you ghost your bills or treat them with respect.

Most lenders want to see a credit score of **at least** 620 for a conventional loan. A higher score (think 740 and up) means better interest rates, which means you'll pay less for your home over time. A lower score? That means higher interest rates—or worse, no loan at all.

How to Boost Your Credit Score Before Buying a Home:

▸ **Pay your bills on time.** (Like, actually on time. Every time.)

▸ **Keep your credit utilization low.** (Aim for under 30% of your limit.)

▸ **Don't open new lines of credit right before applying for a loan.** (No, now is NOT the time for a new car or a shopping spree.)

▸ **Dispute any errors on your credit report.** (Yes, mistakes happen, and they can hurt you.)

Not sure what your credit score is? It's time to check. Sites like Credit Karma or your bank's online portal can give you a snapshot. If it's looking rough, don't panic. You can improve it—it just takes time and discipline.

3. Budgeting for Homeownership: Not Just the Mortgage (Hello, Hidden Costs!)

So, you've used a mortgage calculator online and figured out what you think you can afford. *Cute.* But let's talk about the real cost of homeownership, because your mortgage payment is only part of the story.

What You'll Be Paying For:

▸ **Mortgage Payment** – The big one. But remember, this isn't just your home loan—it includes interest, too.

▸ **Property Taxes** – Depending on where you live, these can add hundreds (or even thousands) to your monthly costs.

▸ **Homeowners Insurance** – Unlike renters insurance, this one isn't optional. And if you're in a flood or earthquake zone? More money.

▸ **Maintenance & Repairs** – Stuff breaks. A lot. Experts recommend setting aside 1-3% of your home's value per year for maintenance.

- **HOA Fees** – If you're buying in a neighborhood with a home-owners association, congratulations! You now have another bill to pay.
- **Utilities & Bills** – Heating, cooling, water, trash, internet—it all adds up.
- **The Oh-Crap Fund (aka Emergency Savings for Homeowners)** — New homeowners quickly learn that houses have a way of surprising you. That surprise is rarely a good one. The HVAC system will die in the middle of summer, the roof will leak right before a storm, or your water heater will decide it's time for a flood.

To avoid panicked Googling at 2 AM, you need a home emergency fund. Aim for at least 3 to 6 months' worth of expenses saved up before buying a home. Trust me, future you will thank you.

4. The Homebuying Budget Worksheet

(Can You Afford This Adventure?)

This is the part where you get real with your finances. Before jumping into house hunting, fill out this worksheet to see if you're truly ready.

Monthly Income

Take-Home Pay: $_____

Other Monthly Income: $_____

Total Monthly Income: $_____

Monthly Expenses (Before Homeownership)

Rent: $_____

Car Payment & Insurance: $_____

Phone & Internet: $_____

Groceries & Dining Out: $_____

Fun Money: $_____

Credit Card & Other Debt Payments: $_____

Total Monthly Expenses: $_____

Future Homeownership Costs

Estimated Mortgage Payment: $_____

Property Taxes: $_____

Homeowners Insurance: $_____

Utilities & Bills: $_____

Maintenance Fund (1-3% of home value/year): $_____

Total Homeownership Costs: $_____

Savings Check

Current Savings for Down Payment: $_____

Closing Costs Savings: $_____

Emergency Fund: $_____

Final Question: Do you have enough savings AND can you comfortably afford all of the above?

☐ **YES!** Let's do this!

☐ **NO!** Okay, let's make a plan to get there.

Final Thoughts: Is It Time to Buy, or Should You Keep Saving?

If you filled out the worksheet and realized you're financially rock solid, great! Time to move on to the fun part—house hunting.

If you came up short, don't be discouraged. The worst thing you can do is rush into homeownership when you're not financially ready. Keep saving, keep improving your credit, and keep learning. When the time is right, you'll be able to buy with confidence (and without panic).

House It Done?

Buying a home isn't just about having enough money to buy—it's about having enough money to keep the home without losing sleep. Take the time to prepare, and future-you will be so grateful.

CHAPTER 2

The Real Costs of Owning a Home

(Surprise! It's Not Just the Mortgage Payment)

So, you've crunched the numbers, high-fived yourself for affording a mortgage, and started imagining your life as a homeowner. Maybe you've even started looking at Pinterest boards full of dreamy kitchen remodels. But before you start planning your first dinner party, let's talk about the part of homeownership that no one brags about on Instagram: all the random, soul-sucking, wallet-draining costs that come with owning a home. Yes, that monthly mortgage payment is a biggie. But it's just the beginning. Welcome to The Real Costs of Owning a Home, where your money will disappear faster than you can say, *"Wait, how much for a water heater?"*

1. Property Taxes: The Bill That Never Stops Coming

Your mortgage payment may feel huge, but guess what? The government also wants a piece of the action. Property taxes are what you pay to your city, county, or state for the privilege of owning real estate, and they're based on your home's value.

Here's the fun part: Property taxes never really go away. Even when you've paid off your house, you'll still owe them. It's like a lifelong subscription to homeownership, but instead of getting a fun magazine, you get a bill.

How Much Are Property Taxes?

It depends on where you live. Some states have low property taxes (hi, Hawaii!), while others (*cough* New Jersey *cough*) will make you question all your life choices.

- Property tax rates are usually a percentage of your home's assessed value.
- Most homeowners pay between 1% and 3% of their home's value annually in property taxes.
- This means if your house is worth $300,000, you could be paying anywhere from $3,000 to $9,000 per year—or $250 to $750 per month—on top of your mortgage.

How to Prepare for Property Taxes

- **Check the tax rate before buying a home.** That dream house might look affordable, but crazy property taxes could ruin the deal. Some property taxes also have extra local assessments.
- **See if you qualify for exemptions.** Some states offer discounts for veterans, seniors, or first-time homeowners.
- **Factor it into your monthly payments.** Your lender may roll your taxes into your mortgage (called an *escrow or impound account*), so you don't have to worry about a surprise tax bill.

2. HOA Fees: Paying to Follow the Rules

If you're buying a home in a community with a homeowners association (HOA), congratulations! You now have to pay another bill.

HOAs maintain shared spaces, enforce community rules (or C,C&Rs), and sometimes make questionable decisions about what color you can paint your front door.

HOA Fees Can Range From Reasonable to Ridiculous

- ▸ **Low-end:** $50–$100/month *(basic maintenance, maybe a pool).*
- ▸ **Mid-range:** $200–$500/month *(gated community, landscaping, maybe security).*
- ▸ **High-end:** $1,000+/month *(fancy amenities, golf courses, security guards who sit in a tower)*

Before buying a home in an HOA community, ask these important questions:

- ✓ **What are the monthly fees?** Can you afford them?
- ✓ **What do they cover?** Some HOAs include trash pickup, some include water, landscaping, and maintenance. Others just exist to send angry letters about your lawn.
- ✓ **Are there special assessments?** Sometimes, HOAs charge extra fees for big projects *(hello, surprise roof replacement fees!)*

Moral of the story: Don't just look at the house—look at the HOA rules, account reserves, and costs, too.

3. Utilities & Monthly Bills: The Bare Necessities (That Cost a Lot)

Remember when you were a renter, and your landlord covered some of the utilities? **Those days are over.** Now, every time you take a long, hot shower, you're literally washing money down the drain. (This is just an estimate—actual costs may vary depending on how much your home guzzles water and electricity. *Got a lush garden that demands daily hydration like a diva houseplant or a hot tub that keeps your electric meter spinning like a Vegas slot machine?* Yeah, all of that can crank up your bills. So, take these numbers with a spark of reality).

Common Utility Costs:

▸ **Electricity:** $100–$300/month
▸ **Gas (Heating):** $50–$200/month (higher in winter!)
▸ **Water & Sewer:** $50–$400*/month (*landscape dependent)
▸ **Trash & Recycling:** $30–$50/month
▸ **Internet & Cable:** $100–$300/month (and yet, your WiFi still cuts out)

How to Avoid Bill Shock:

▸ **Ask the current homeowners for an estimate of average utility costs.**
▸ **Look into energy-efficient appliances and smart thermostats.**
▸ **Brace yourself for seasonal fluctuations.** Your AC and heater will be your best friends *and* worst enemies.

4. Home Maintenance & Repairs: The Oh-Crap Fund

Owning a home means you're in charge of fixing everything. There's no landlord to call. It's just you, your wallet, and a desperate Google search for *"why is my fridge making that noise?"*

Regular Maintenance Costs

Home experts recommend setting aside 1–3% of your home's value per year for maintenance.

- If your home is worth $300,000, you should plan on spending $3,000–$9,000 per year on repairs.
- Some years will be easy (just basic upkeep).
- Other years, your water heater will explode.

Common Expenses That Sneak Up on Homeowners:

- **Plumbing Issues**—A leaky pipe can turn into a $5,000 repair *real quick*.
- **HVAC Maintenance**—Your AC and furnace need yearly checkups ($100–$300 each).
- **Roof Repairs**—Replacing a roof can cost $8,000–$20,000 (start saving now).
- **Appliance Replacements**—Fridges, ovens, and dishwashers don't last forever.

Pro Tip:

- ✓ Get a home warranty for your first year. It might cover major repairs.
- ✓ Set up an emergency fund for home expenses. It's not *if* something breaks—it's *when*.

5. The Home Emergency Fund: Because Things <u>WILL</u> Break

Owning a home without an emergency fund is like going on a road trip with no gas money—it's **not going to end well.**

How Much Should You Save?

Minimum: 3 months' worth of expenses (bare minimum).

Better: 6 months' worth of expenses (comfort zone).

Best: 12 months' worth of expenses (if you want to sleep peacefully).

Put your emergency fund in a high-yield savings account where you can access it quickly. This is not money for vacations. This is "oh-crap-the-roof-is-leaking" money.

Can You Afford to Own a Home?

Yes, homeownership builds wealth. Yes, it's an amazing investment. But it's also expensive, unpredictable, and occasionally exhausting.

Before you jump in, make sure you're not just *mortgage-ready*—you're homeownership-ready. That means planning for:

- ✓ Property taxes and HOA fees
- ✓ Utility and maintenance costs
- ✓ Emergency repairs (*because something WILL break*)
- ✓ A home emergency fund

If you're financially prepared for *all* these costs, then congratulations! You're truly ready for homeownership.

House It Done?

Homeownership is a wild ride, but if you're prepared for the hidden costs, you'll be able to enjoy it without financial panic. So start saving, budget wisely, and welcome to the club.

CHAPTER 3

The Great Home Hunt

(Aka: Swiping Right on Zillow)

So, you're financially ready to buy a home. You've got a solid credit score, a down payment saved, and an emergency fund tucked away for the inevitable *oops* moments of homeownership. Bravo! Now comes the fun part—house hunting!

Or at least, it *should* be fun. But if you've ever spent hours scrolling Zillow at 2 AM, convinced you've found "the one," only to see it go pending 15 minutes later, you know that house hunting can feel like a mix between speed dating and The Hunger Games.

But don't worry—I've got you. In this chapter, we'll break down:

▸ The different types of homes and how to pick the right one
▸ The house-hunting process (aka: what NOT to do)
▸ Red flags to watch for when touring homes
▸ Why you need a real estate agent (spoiler: because we save you from bad decisions)
▸ How to set realistic expectations (*aka: Champagne dreams on a beer budget*)

Happy House Hunting!

1. What Kind of Home is Right for You?

Before you start swiping through listings, you need to figure out what kind of home actually fits your lifestyle. There's more than one type of property out there, and they all come with pros and cons.

Single-Family Home

- ✓ You get a yard, privacy, and no shared walls.
- ✗ More maintenance (hello, mowing the lawn and fixing the roof).

Condo

- ✓ Less maintenance (HOA handles the exterior).
- ✗ You'll have HOA fees and possibly *very opinionated* neighbors.

Townhouse

- ✓ More space than a condo, but with shared walls.
- ✗ Some maintenance responsibilities, depending on the HOA.

Fixer-Upper

- ✓ Usually cheaper upfront, potential for profit.
- ✗ Requires time, money, and possibly a therapist.

New Construction

- ✓ Brand new everything, minimal maintenance.
- ✗ Might be more expensive, and you'll wait months to move in.

Acreage/Rural Property

- ✓ Peace, quiet, and maybe some chickens.
- ✗ A *lot* of upkeep, and good luck getting Uber Eats delivered.

> **Pro Tip:**
>
> Make a list of your *non-negotiables* (must-haves) and your *nice-to-haves*. This will keep you from falling in love with a cute house that actually makes no sense for your lifestyle.

2. The House-Hunting Process (aka: Avoid These Rookie Mistakes)

Most people think house hunting is just scrolling listings and going to open houses. If only it were that simple! Here's how to do it *right*:

Step 1: Get Pre-Approved

If you're not pre-approved for a mortgage, you're not ready to shop. A pre-approval tells you *exactly* how much house you can afford and makes sellers take you seriously. If you've got the cash, then congrats—you can pass GO, collect your keys, and skip the financing hurdles.

> ✕ **What not to do:** Start looking at homes *before* getting pre-approved. This is how heartbreak happens when you fall in love with a house you can't afford.

Step 2: Hire a Real Estate Agent (Yes, You Need One!)

I know, I know—you think you can do this alone because Zillow exists. But a good agent will:

- ✓ Find homes that fit your needs (before they hit the market!)
- ✓ Schedule showings and help you avoid bad deals
- ✓ Handle negotiations (so you don't overpay or get stuck with a lemon)
- ✓ Guide you through inspections, appraisals, and *all* the paperwork

Shameless Plug: A great real estate agent (like yours truly 😊) can save you thousands of dollars and endless headaches. We also know what red flags to look for—more on that next.

3. Red Flags to Watch for When Touring Homes

Just because a home *looks* pretty doesn't mean it's a good buy. Pay attention to these warning signs:

- ✓ **Cracks in the Foundation** – Some hairline cracks are normal, but large gaps = *big trouble.*
- ✓ **Water Stains or Mold** – A sign of leaks and possible expensive repairs.
- ✓ **Strange Smells** – If a home smells *musty* or *like Febreze overload,* they're hiding something.
- ✓ **Doors & Windows That Don't Close Properly** – Could be foundation issues (aka: $$$).
- ✓ **Fresh Paint in Odd Places** – Could be covering up damage.
- ✓ **Flipped Homes That Look Rushed** – If the remodel looks sloppy, the work underneath might be worse.

Pro Tip:

Always hire a home inspector. Even if the house *looks* perfect, an inspector can uncover issues that could cost you big time.

4. Setting Realistic Expectations (aka: Champagne Dreams on a Beer Budget)

One of the hardest parts of house hunting is realizing that your dream home might be out of your budget. Here's how to keep your expectations in check:

The Pinterest Effect

You want a *fully remodeled* house with a gourmet kitchen and spa bathroom, but your budget says *1970s time capsule with wood paneling*. Compromises will be made.

HGTV Lies to You

No, you *probably* won't find a perfectly updated home for a steal. Homes on HGTV are staged, edited, and sometimes *outright fake*.

Size vs. Location

You might be able to get a bigger house if you move farther from the city. But is that extra square footage worth an hour-long commute every day? Think about it—your car might become your second home. Seriously, consider how this could impact your sanity (and your podcast playlist).

Compromise, But Don't Settle

You can change the paint color, flooring, and fixtures—but you *can't* change the location or the floor plan. Focus on the things that actually matter.

Final Thoughts: The Key to a Stress-Free House Hunt

House hunting can be exhilarating, frustrating, and slightly exhausting. But if you go in prepared, you'll save yourself a lot of stress (and maybe even some money).

Key Takeaways:

- ✓ **Know what you can afford** before you start looking.
- ✓ **Hire a real estate agent** to help you find the right home and negotiate a good deal.
- ✓ **Pay attention to red flags** when touring homes.
- ✓ **Be realistic about your budget** and what you can get.

If you follow these tips, you'll *actually* enjoy the house-hunting process instead of wanting to throw your phone at the wall after another Zillow disappointment.

House It Done?

Finding the right home is like dating—if you rush into it, you might end up with something that *looks* good but isn't actually the right fit. Take your time, trust the process, and when you find "the one," you'll know.

CHAPTER 4

How to Make an Offer They Can't Refuse

So, you've found *the one*. The house that checks all your boxes, makes your heart skip a beat, and has you mentally rearranging furniture before you even leave the showing. Now comes the tricky part—actually getting it.

In a competitive market, submitting an offer isn't just about throwing out a number and hoping for the best. It's about strategy. Sellers are looking for the best overall offer, not just the highest price. And with multiple buyers eyeing the same house, you need to put your best foot (and wallet) forward from the start.

Let's break down how to submit an offer that not only gets noticed but also gets accepted.

Step 1: Know the Seller's Priorities

Not every seller is just looking for the highest offer. Sometimes, other factors can be just as important:

- ✓ **Fast closing** – They want to move ASAP.
- ✓ **Leaseback option** – They need time to find their next home.

✓ **Fewer contingencies** – They don't want the deal to fall apart over financing or inspections.

✓ **Strong financing** – They need a buyer who won't back out due to loan issues.

Your agent can **communicate with the listing agent** to get inside info on what's most important to the seller. This intel can help shape your offer to align with their needs.

Step 2: Make Your Offer Stand Out

Here's what makes an offer go from "meh" to "let's accept this one!"

Get Pre-Approved or Bring Cash to the Party

A pre-approval letter (not just a pre-qualification) shows sellers that you're financially solid and ready to close. Want to take it up a notch? Some lenders offer fully underwritten pre-approvals, making your offer almost as strong as cash. Going all cash? Great—but be ready to prove it. Sellers will expect a proof of funds statement from your bank to confirm you actually have the money to close. No Monopoly money allowed!

Offer a Strong (and Realistic) Price

In a multiple-offer situation, offering below asking price isn't going to cut it.

How to decide on your offer price:

▸ If the house is priced right, consider offering full price or slightly above.

▸ If the home is underpriced to create a bidding war, expect to go higher.

▸ If it's overpriced, tread carefully—overpaying out of desperation is a risky move.

Your agent will analyze comparable sales (comps) to help you make an informed decision.

Offer a Bigger Earnest Money Deposit

Earnest money is your good faith deposit, showing the seller you're serious. Standard amounts are 1-3% of the home price, but bumping this up can make your offer stand out.

Pro Tip:

Earnest money still goes toward your down payment—it's just front-loaded to make your offer more attractive.

Consider an Appraisal Gap Clause

In hot markets, homes often sell for more than the appraised value, which can be an issue if you're financing. An appraisal gap clause tells the seller you'll cover the difference or up to a certain amount if the appraisal comes in low. **Warning:** Only do this if you have the cash to cover it!

Keep Contingencies Light (But Don't Waive What You Need!)

Contingencies protect you, but too many can scare off sellers. Here's how to strike a balance:

- ✓ **Financing Contingency:** Needed if you're getting a loan—don't waive this unless you're absolutely sure.
- ✓ **Inspection Contingency:** Instead of waiving it completely, consider keeping the inspection but limiting repair requests to major structural or safety issues. This shows the seller you're serious while still protecting you from unexpected (and expensive) surprises.

✓ **Appraisal Contingency:** If you can cover a gap, consider modifying this instead of waiving it completely.

Step 3: Sweeten the Deal Without Overpaying

Sometimes, it's the little things that help you win:

Be Flexible on Closing Date

If the seller needs extra time to move, offering a rent-back (letting them stay after closing for a short period) could put your offer on top.

Cover Small Costs

Offering to pay for a home warranty, title insurance, or some seller closing costs can make your offer stronger without breaking the bank.

Limit Requests for Extras

Asking for the patio furniture, washer/dryer, or fridge in a bidding war? *Not the best move.* Keep your offer clean and focused on the house itself.

Step 4: What About Cash Offers?

You've heard it before: **"Cash is king."** But is it really?

Cash offers can be stronger, but they're not always the winner. If a cash buyer is offering less than a financed buyer, a seller might still go with the higher offer—especially if they know the financed offer is solid.

The advantage of cash buyers? They can close quickly and aren't tied to loan approvals or appraisals.

Step 5: What Happens After You Submit?

Here's what could happen after you send in your offer:

The Seller Accepts Your Offer

Congrats! Now you move into the next phase—inspections, final loan approval, and closing.

The Seller Counters Your Offer

They might tweak price, contingencies, or closing date. If this happens, you can:

▶ **Accept** their changes

▶ **Counter back**

▶ **Walk away** if it's not a good deal

You Get Outbid

It happens. Don't take it personally. Ask your agent what made the winning offer stronger and use that information next time.

Winning Without Losing Your Sanity

Submitting an offer—especially in a multiple-offer situation—can feel like a high-stakes poker game. But with the right strategy, strong financing, and a clean offer, you'll be in the best position to win.

House It Done?

Submitting the best offer takes strategy, timing, and a little bit of luck. Stay prepared, stay flexible, **and remember**—if you lose one, there's always another home out there. Your dream home might just be the next one you see.

CHAPTER 5

Escrow, Inspections & All the Things No One Warned You About

(Aka: The Part Where You Question All Your Life Choices)

Congratulations! You made an offer on a house, and the seller actually said **YES**. You did it. You're under contract. Go ahead and celebrate, but not too much—because now comes the part where the universe decides to test your patience, finances, and sanity all at once.

Welcome to **Escrow**, a strange, mysterious period where your dream home is *technically* yours... but also not. This is the homebuying purgatory where your bank, title company, inspectors, and real estate agent all team up to make sure everything is in order before you officially get the keys.

Escrow is where deals can fall apart, unexpected problems arise, and buyers develop a nervous twitch from all the waiting. But don't worry— I'll walk you through it so you come out the other side with both your sanity and your future home intact.

What is Escrow, and Why Does It Take Forever?

Escrow is the holding period between having an accepted offer and actually closing on your home. Think of it like ordering something online, but instead of arriving in two days (thanks, Amazon), it takes 30 to 45 days (or longer, if the universe hates you).

What Happens During Escrow?

- **Your earnest money is deposited** – This is the "good faith" deposit you put down to show you're serious about buying the house.
- **The home gets inspected** – To make sure you're not buying a money pit.
- **The home gets appraised** – Your lender wants to make sure the home is actually worth what you're paying for it.
- **Your lender finalizes your loan** – The bank double-checks your finances, employment, and credit score (again) before approving the loan.
- **Title search and insurance are completed** – To make sure no one else can claim ownership of the property.
- **Lots and lots of paperwork** – You will sign your name more times than you ever have in your life.

Why Does It Feel Like It's Taking Forever?

- **Lenders are slow.** They have to verify every financial detail of your life.
- **Inspections and appraisals take time.** You're at the mercy of other people's schedules.
- **Paperwork gets stuck in limbo.** Sometimes a small missing document can delay the whole process.

▶ **Waiting on HOA documents.** If your home is in an HOA, get comfy—those docs can take forever. Some HOA's move at lightning speed (rare), while others seem to operate by carrier pigeon. Either way, you don't want to close without seeing them first!

Pro Tip:

Do NOT make any big financial moves during escrow. Don't open new credit cards, don't buy a new car, and don't quit your job. Your lender is watching, and they *will* pull your financing.

The Inspection Process: What to Freak Out About vs. What to Ignore

Home inspections are where dreams meet reality. This is the part where a professional walks through your future home and tells you *everything* that's wrong with it. And trust me, every home has issues.

What Inspections Cover:

▶ Structural integrity (foundation, roof, walls)
▶ Electrical system (because fire hazards are bad)
▶ Plumbing (leaks, water pressure, drainage)
▶ HVAC (heating & cooling—unless you enjoy sweating/freezing)
▶ Pest infestations (termites, rodents, general unwanted guests)

Your inspector will give you a detailed report listing all the problems they found. This is where most buyers start to panic—but let's break it down.

What to Freak Out About (a.k.a. Deal Breakers)

- ✓ Major foundation cracks (because fixing it costs a fortune)
- ✓ Electrical hazards
- ✓ A roof that needs immediate replacement (that's $10K–$20K you weren't planning on spending)
- ✓ Termite or mold infestations (because ew, and also expensive)
- ✓ Plumbing disasters

What NOT to Freak Out About (a.k.a. Normal Homeowner Stuff)

- ✓ Peeling paint
- ✓ A door that sticks (*WD-40 exists for a reason*)
- ✓ Cosmetic updates
- ✓ Minor cracks in drywall (*literally every house has these*)
- ✓ Outdated appliances (*annoying, but not a deal-breaker*)

Pro Tip:

No home is perfect. The goal of an inspection isn't to scare you—it's to make sure there aren't *major* issues that could financially ruin you.

Negotiating Repairs Without Losing Your Mind

So, your inspection report came back, and—surprise!—your future home has *some* issues. Now it's time to negotiate with the seller.

Your Four Options:

1. Ask the seller to fix things before closing.
2. Ask for a credit at closing (so you can fix things yourself).
3. Accept the home as-is (only if the issues are minor).

4. Combination request of the above.

What You *Should* Ask the Seller to Fix:

▸ Major safety issues (electrical hazards, plumbing failures, etc.)
▸ Structural issues (foundation cracks, bad roof, etc.)
▸ Broken appliances that were included in the sale.

What You *Should NOT* Ask the Seller to Fix:

Small cosmetic issues (paint, scratches, minor dings)

Things you *should have noticed* before making an offer

Stuff under $100 (pick your battles)

Pro Tip:

Be reasonable. Asking a seller to replace every tiny thing will only annoy them. If you really want the home, focus on the *big stuff* and let go of the rest.

The Final Walk-Through: Last Chance to Catch Problems

The final walk-through happens normally 1- 5 days before closing. This is your **last chance** to make sure everything is in order before signing the paperwork.

What to Check:

✓ **Repairs:** Did the seller actually fix what they promised?
✓ **Utilities:** Is the water running? Do the lights work?
✓ **Appliances:** Are the included appliances still in the home and functioning?

✓ **Leaks:** Check under sinks and ceilings for any signs of new water damage.

✓ **Doors & Windows:** Do they open and close properly?

If something is wrong, speak up NOW. Once you sign those closing papers, any problems are officially your responsibility.

Pro Tip:

Bring your inspection report to the final walk-through. Use it as a checklist to make sure everything looks good.

Surviving Escrow Without Losing Your Mind

Escrow and inspections can be stressful, but they're designed to protect you from making a bad investment.

Key Takeaways:

▸ **Escrow takes time.** Be patient.

▸ **Inspections will reveal issues.** Focus on the big stuff.

▸ **Negotiate repairs,** but don't nitpick.

▸ **Do a thorough final walk-through before closing.**

Once you survive this stage, **you're almost there**—the keys to your new home are just around the corner!

House It Done?

Escrow is like the final test before homeownership. It's annoying, stressful, and full of paperwork—but once you get through it, you'll officially own a home. And trust me, it'll all be worth it when you get those keys in your hand.

CHAPTER 6

Closing Day: Sign, Seal, Celebrate!

(Spoiler: You'll Need a Drink After This)

You did it. You made it through house hunting, the emotional rollercoaster of escrow, the dreaded inspection negotiations, and now—you're at the finish line. Closing day.

This is the big moment—the official transition into homeownership. But before you pop the champagne, let's talk about what really happens at the closing. In some states, you'll gather around an actual closing table; in others, it's just signing paperwork separately. Either way, it's not quite as simple as showing up, grabbing keys, and riding off into your happily-ever-after.

Nope. There's still one more round of paperwork, fees, and last-minute stress before you can finally claim your home. But don't worry—I'll walk you through it.

1. Understanding Closing Costs (Yep, More Money)

Just when you thought you were done handing over money, closing costs show up like an uninvited guest at your victory party.

What Are Closing Costs?

Closing costs are the fees associated with finalizing your mortgage and transferring ownership of the home. Expect to pay 2% to 5% of the home's purchase price in closing costs.

So if you bought a $300,000 home, that's anywhere from $6,000 to $15,000 extra in fees. Fun, right?

What's Included in Closing Costs?

Here's where all that money is going:

- ✓ **Loan Origination Fee** – What your lender charges to process your mortgage.
- ✓ **Appraisal Fee** – What you paid to confirm the home's value.
- ✓ **Title Insurance & Title Search** – Protects you from ownership disputes.
- ✓ **Property Taxes** – You may need to prepay a few months' worth.
- ✓ **Homeowners Insurance** – Most lenders require the first year paid upfront.
- ✓ **Recording Fees & Other Legal Costs** – Because the government wants a cut, too.

Pro Tip:

Always ask your lender for a **Closing Disclosure** at least three days before closing. This document breaks down your exact closing costs, so you're not caught off guard.

2. Signing a Stack of Papers Taller Than You

Depending on your state, on or before closing day, you'll sit down at a big table with:

▸ A notary
▸ Your real estate agent (sometimes)
▸ Your lender (sometimes)
▸ The title company (sometimes)
▸ Possibly the sellers (but often, they sign separately)
▸ And then... you sign **everything**.

The Mountain of Paperwork Includes:

▸ **The Promissory Note** – The document that says, "Yes, I agree to owe the bank money for the next 15–30 years."
▸ **The Mortgage/Deed of Trust** – The agreement giving the lender the right to foreclose if you don't pay.
▸ **The Closing Disclosure** – The final breakdown of your loan terms and closing costs.
▸ **The Deed** – The document officially transferring ownership of the home to you.

Reality Check: This part takes about an hour, and your hand will cramp from all the signatures. Some of the documents will feel repetitive, and most of them will be written in confusing legal jargon. Just smile, nod, and if you have any questions call your real estate agent or lender.

Pro Tip:

Read the fine print on your loan documents. Your mortgage interest rate, term length, and monthly payment amount should match what your lender originally promised. If anything looks wrong, speak up before signing!

3. When You Officially Get the Keys (But Don't Expect to Move In That Day)

Once you've signed all the papers, your next question is:

"Where are my keys?!"

Here's the thing—just because you signed doesn't mean you can move in immediately.

When Do You Actually Get the Keys?

Same Day – If your loan has already been funded, you'll get the keys *right after title confirms the closing.*

Next Business Day – If the funds haven't cleared yet, you'll have to wait.

Delayed Closing – If there are last-minute funding or title issues, it could take a *few days* longer.

> **Pro Tip:**
>
> Don't schedule movers on closing day. There's always a small chance of delays, and you don't want to be stuck with a moving truck and nowhere to put your stuff.

Final Thoughts: The Moment You've Been Waiting For

Closing day might feel like a legal obstacle course, but when it's all said and done, you're officially a homeowner!

Key Takeaways:

- **Closing costs are real** (and expensive)—budget for them.
- **Signing paperwork takes about an hour** (and a lot of hand strength).
- **You may not get the keys immediately**—be patient!

Once you have those keys in your hand, go celebrate! Pop the champagne, take a victory lap through your new home, and start planning how you'll make it yours.

House It Done?

Owning a home is one of the biggest milestones of your life—so enjoy the moment. You worked hard for this. Now, go take a million pictures in front of your new front door like the proud homeowner you are.

CHAPTER 7

Welcome Home! Now What?

(Keeping Your Home from Falling Apart)

Pop the champagne! *You did it.* You survived the house hunt, offers, escrow, inspections, and closing. You have the keys to your very own home. Take a moment to soak that all in.

Now, before you get too comfortable, let me hit you with some reality:

Homes don't take care of themselves.

Sure, your house looks perfect *now*, but give it six months without maintenance, and suddenly, your gutters are clogged, your HVAC is gasping for life, and your water heater is staging a rebellion.

This chapter is all about keeping your home in tip-top shape so you're not drowning in expensive repairs down the road.

1. Routine Maintenance Must-Dos (And Why Ignoring Them Is a Bad Idea)

Owning a home is kind of like owning a car—if you don't maintain it, it'll break down at the worst possible time. And unlike renting, there's no landlord to call when things go south.

Ignoring maintenance = *expensive consequences.*

Here's what happens when you put off basic upkeep:

- ✓ **Skip HVAC maintenance?** Get ready for a broken AC in the middle of summer.
- ✓ **Don't clean your gutters?** Enjoy your new indoor waterfall from a leaky roof.
- ✓ **Forget to check for leaks?** Say hello to mold (and thousands in repairs).
- ✓ **Neglect your water heater?** Congrats, you just bought yourself an emergency cold shower.

Pro Tip:

Regular maintenance may not be fun, but it saves you thousands in the long run.

2. Home Warranty vs. Homeowners Insurance (What's the Difference?)

A lot of new homeowners mix these up, so let's set the record straight.

Homeowners Insurance (Required by Your Lender)

Covers **major disasters** like:

- ▶ Fire
- ▶ Storm damage
- ▶ Theft
- ▶ Some types of water damage (not floods—those require separate insurance)

Home Warranty (Optional, But Useful)

Covers **breakdowns of home systems and appliances** due to normal wear and tear, like:

- HVAC system
- Plumbing leaks
- Water heater
- Kitchen appliances

Do You Need a Home Warranty?

If your home is brand new or has updated appliances, you probably don't need one. But if you bought an older home with aging systems, a home warranty can save you from big repair bills in your first few years.

> **Pro Tip:**
>
> Home warranties can be *hit or miss*—and a total pain in the a**. Read the fine print carefully, because some cover next to nothing, while others *might* be worth it. It's basically a part-time job just to get your leaky water heater fixed. Fun times!

3. DIY Fixes vs When to Call a Pro

Owning a home means you'll have to fix things. The question is: should you DIY it, or call a pro?

Here's a handy guide:

DIY

- ✓ **Patching small holes in walls** (Go for it, *spackle and paint are cheap!*)

✓ **Replacing air filters** (*Seriously, do this every 3 months!*)
✓ **Unclogging a drain**
✓ **Painting rooms** (*Just tape off the edges unless you like the "abstract art" look.*)

Call a Pro (Unless You Want a Disaster)

✓ **Electrical work** (Unless you enjoy power outages.)
✓ **Major plumbing issues** (A leaky pipe can become a flood real quick.)
✓ **Roof repairs** (One wrong move and you're looking at a hospital bill, too.)
✓ **Foundation problems** (If your house is shifting, you need a specialist—not YouTube.)

Pro Tip:

DIY what you can, but don't be afraid to call in the experts for anything structural, electrical, or plumbing-related. A cheap DIY mistake can end up costing more in repairs.

4. Home Maintenance Schedule (Monthly, Quarterly, & Annual Tasks)

To help you stay on top of things, here's a home maintenance checklist broken down into monthly, quarterly, and annual tasks.

Monthly Home Maintenance

▸ Change HVAC filters
▸ Test smoke & carbon monoxide detectors
▸ Check for leaks under sinks
▸ Clean out your garbage disposal (ice + lemon peel = fresh and clean!)
▸ Inspect your HVAC vents for dust buildup

Quarterly (Every 3 Months)

▶ Clean gutters (especially after heavy rain!)

▶ Inspect plumbing for minor leaks

▶ Deep clean kitchen appliances

▶ Check your water softener (if you have one)

Annual Home Maintenance

▶ Service your HVAC system before summer/winter

▶ Drain & flush the water heater (*removes sediment buildup!*)

▶ Power wash the exterior of your home

▶ Check the roof for damage or missing shingles

▶ Reseal windows and doors to prevent drafts

Pro Tip:

Set calendar reminders for these tasks so you actually do them!

Welcome to Homeownership!

Owning a home is exciting, rewarding, and slightly terrifying all at once. But if you keep up with maintenance and plan ahead for repairs, your home will stay in great shape for years to come.

Key Takeaways:

▶ Regular maintenance saves you money (and headaches).

▶ Homeowners insurance and home warranties are NOT the same.

▶ Some things you can DIY, but some require a pro.

▶ Follow a maintenance schedule to avoid costly surprises.

Now, go enjoy your new home—just don't forget to check the air filters first. 😊

House It Done?

Buying a home is only the beginning. The real challenge? Keeping it from falling apart. Stay on top of maintenance, know when to call a pro, and—most importantly—enjoy your new place!

CHAPTER 8

The Investment Property Game

(How to Afford a Second One Without Selling a Kidney)

So, you've conquered homeownership. You've changed the air filters, dealt with a minor plumbing issue, and survived your first surprise property tax bill. And now, you're starting to wonder...

"What if I bought another house?"

Maybe you want a vacation home. Maybe you want to become a landlord. Or maybe you're just dreaming of a passive income stream so you can sip cocktails on a beach while your properties make money for you.

Whatever the reason, buying an investment property can be a game-changer for building wealth—but it can also be a financial disaster if you don't do it right.

In this chapter, we'll cover:

- ✓ When (and why) to buy a second home or rental property
- ✓ How rental income *actually* works (hint: it's not 100% profit)

✓ Fixer-upper vs. turnkey properties—what's the better investment?

✓ The tax benefits of owning multiple properties

Let's dive in!

1. When and Why to Buy an Investment Property

Buying an investment property is not the same as buying your primary home. It's not about emotions—it's about numbers. Before you jump in, ask yourself:

Do I have at least 15-20% for a down payment?

▶ Investment property loans require larger down payments than primary homes.

Do I have enough savings for unexpected expenses?

▶ Rentals come with surprise repairs (because tenants never call about the *small* stuff).

Can I handle the responsibilities of being a landlord?

▶ Dealing with late rent payments, broken toilets, and weird tenant complaints isn't for everyone.

If you answered **yes** to these, then it might be time to start looking for your next property.

Why Consider Buying an Investment Property?

✓ **Extra Income** – Rental properties can create a steady cash flow each month.

✓ **Long-Term Appreciation** – Real estate generally increases in value over time.

✓ **Diversified Investments** – Owning property adds to your wealth beyond stocks & savings.

✓ **Tax Benefits** – Mortgage interest, depreciation, and maintenance costs may be deductible.

Pro Tip:

Don't buy an investment property just because it sounds fun. Make sure the numbers work before making any moves.

2. Understanding Rental Income & Expenses

Most new investors think, "If my mortgage is $1,500 and I charge $2,000 in rent, I make $500 a month!" *Wrong*.

There are a lot of extra costs to factor in. **Let's break it down:**

Typical Rental Property Expenses

▸ **Mortgage Payment** – Principal + interest + property taxes + insurance.

▸ **HOA Fees (if applicable)** – Some properties come with costly monthly fees.

▸ **Maintenance & Repairs** – A/C units die. Toilets clog. Tenants break things. Expect to spend at least 10% of rental income on maintenance.

▸ **Property Management Fees** – If you don't want to deal with tenants, a property manager will—for a fee (usually 8-12% of rent).

▸ **Vacancy Costs** – Assume your property will be empty for at least one month per year.

The 1% Rule: Does the Property Cash Flow?

A good rule of thumb is the 1% Rule:

Your monthly rent should be at least 1% of the purchase price.

For example:

▶ If you buy a house for $200,000, it should rent for at least $2,000 per month to be a good investment.

Does the 1% Rule always apply? No—but it's a good starting point to see if a property might generate profit.

Pro Tip:

Always run the numbers before buying. If your expected rental income *barely* covers the mortgage, it's not a good investment.

3. Fixer-Upper vs. Turnkey Investment: What's Best for You?

Not all investment properties are created equal. Some need TLC, while others are move-in ready. **Let's compare:**

Fixer-Upper Properties

▶ **Cheaper upfront cost** – You can buy below market value.
▶ **Potential for high returns** – A well-done renovation can increase rental value.
▶ **Requires time & money** – Renovations can be expensive and unpredictable.
▶ **More risk** – Surprise issues = *surprise costs.*

Turnkey Rental Properties

▶ **Ready to rent immediately** – No renovations needed.

- ▸ **Less hassle** – Less stress, fewer surprises.
- ▸ **More expensive upfront** – You pay for convenience.
- ▸ **Smaller profit margins** – Harder to find deals with high returns.

Which One Should You Choose?

If you're handy or experienced with renovations, a fixer-upper can be a great deal. But if you want a stress-free, passive investment, a turnkey rental is the safer bet.

Pro Tip:

Don't underestimate renovation costs. Always budget at least 20-30% extra for unexpected problems.

4. Tax Benefits of Owning Multiple Properties

One of the biggest perks of real estate investing? Tax write-offs.

Here's What You Can Deduct:

- ✓ **Mortgage Interest** – Interest on investment property loans is deductible.
- ✓ **Repairs & Maintenance** – Plumbing fixes, roof repairs, and handyman costs = tax write-offs.
- ✓ **Depreciation** – The IRS lets you depreciate rental property over 27.5 years, reducing taxable income.
- ✓ **Property Management Fees** – Hiring someone to handle tenants? That's deductible.

Bonus: The 1031 Exchange

If you sell an investment property and buy another one, you can defer capital gains taxes using a 1031 exchange. That means you keep more money in your pocket to reinvest.

Pro Tip:

Talk to a tax professional before making investment moves—real estate tax laws are tricky.

Is Real Estate Investing Right for You?

Investing in real estate **can** be a great way to build wealth, but it's **not for everyone.**

Before You Buy, Ask Yourself:

- ▸ **Do I have enough savings for a down payment & emergency expenses?**
- ▸ **Can I handle the responsibilities of being a landlord (or afford property management)?**
- ▸ **Does the property actually generate positive cash flow?**
- ▸ **Am I prepared for the long-term commitment of real estate investing?**

If you're ready, investment properties can be a powerful wealth-building tool. Just make sure you're playing smart, not risky.

House It Done?

Investment properties aren't about *hope*—they're about math. If the numbers don't make sense, walk away. The right deal will come along, and when it does, you'll be ready.

CHAPTER 9
Selling Your Home Like a Pro
(Or At Least Without Losing Your Sanity)

So, you've decided to sell your home. Maybe you're upgrading, downsizing, relocating, or just ready for a change. Whatever the reason, selling a house is not as simple as sticking a "For Sale" sign in the yard and waiting for a buyer to roll in with a suitcase full of cash.

In fact, selling a home can be just as stressful as buying one—if not more. But don't worry! This chapter will walk you through:

✓ Timing the market and pricing your home correctly
✓ The art of staging (aka: strategically hiding your junk)
✓ Negotiating like a boss to get the best deal
✓ The closing process (*yes, again—but now you're a pro*)

Let's get that **SOLD** sign in your yard!

1. Timing the Market & Setting the Right Price

Is Now a Good Time to Sell?

Like everything in real estate, timing matters. If you can be strategic about when you sell, you could make thousands more on your home.

Best Time to Sell: Spring & Early Summer

- ▸ More buyers = more competition = higher offers
- ▸ Families want to move before school starts
- ▸ Warmer weather = homes look better (green grass > dead trees)

Worst Time to Sell: Late Fall & Winter

- ▸ Fewer buyers = lower prices
- ▸ Holidays distract people from house hunting
- ▸ Curb appeal is harder to maintain in winter

Setting the Right Price (Without Scaring Away Buyers)

Pricing your home correctly is the key to selling quickly and for the most money.

- ✓ **Overpricing = No Offers** – If your home sits on the market too long, buyers assume something's wrong with it.
- ✓ **Underpricing = Losing Money** – A low price might attract more buyers, but you could be leaving money on the table.

Pro Tip:

Work with a real estate agent *(hi, that's me!)* to do a Comparative Market Analysis (CMA). This compares your home to recently sold properties in your area to determine a fair market value.

2. The Art of Staging (aka: Hiding All Your Junk)

Want to sell your house faster and for more money? *Staging is the secret weapon.*

Staged homes sell 88% faster and for up to 20% more than un-staged ones. **Why?** Because buyers aren't just looking at a house—they're imagining living in it.

How to Stage Like a Pro (Even If You're Still Living There)

Declutter EVERYTHING.
- ▸ **Rule of Thumb:** If you haven't used it in the last 6 months, pack it up.

Depersonalize the Space.
- ▸ Family photos, political décor, and quirky collections = *distracting*.
- ▸ Buyers need to picture *themselves* in the home, not you.

Let There Be Light!
- ▸ Open blinds, add mirrors, and use warm, inviting lighting.
- ▸ Dark rooms feel smaller—make your home as bright as possible.

Neutral Colors = More Buyers.
- ▸ If your walls are neon green, now is the time to repaint.
- ▸ Stick to light, neutral tones (whites, grays, beiges).

Stage Key Rooms First.
- ▸ **Living Room:** The first impression space. Make it cozy and inviting.
- ▸ **Kitchen:** Clear off countertops, add fresh flowers or a bowl of fruit.
- ▸ **Primary Bedroom:** Neutral bedding, minimal décor, hotel-like feel.

Pro Tip:

If staging sounds overwhelming, consider hiring a professional stager—it's often worth the investment. Expect to pay $2,000-$5,000 for a standard size home.

3. Negotiating Like a Boss

The offers are rolling in—now what?

Don't Just Take the Highest Offer (Look at the Terms!)

Not all offers are created equal. The best offer isn't always the highest price—it's the one with the best terms.

Key Factors to Consider:

- ✓ **Financing Type: Cash offers = may be a faster, smoother closing.** But Cash doesn't always mean commitment!
- ✓ **Contingencies: Fewer contingencies = stronger offer.**
- ✓ **Closing Timeline:** Do you need more time to move? A flexible closing date might be better than a slightly higher price.
- ✓ **Appraisal Waivers:** If a buyer waives the appraisal, there's less risk of a price drop later.

Common Buyer Negotiation Tactics (and How to Respond)

"We love your home, but we want $10K off."

- ▸ *Response:* "Great! Do you also want us to include a unicorn?"
- ▸ *Real Response:* Unless the home is overpriced, stick to your guns—counter at a smaller discount or hold firm.

"We want you to fix EVERYTHING from the inspection."

▶ *Response:* "Absolutely! As long as you'd like to pay an extra $10K."

▶ *Real Response:* Focus on major repairs (roof, HVAC, plumbing) but say no to nitpicky requests.

Pro Tip:

A good real estate agent will handle negotiations to get you the best price **AND** best terms.

4. The Closing Process (Yes, Again—But Now You're a Pro!)

You survived selling negotiations—now it's time for the final round of paperwork.

What Happens During Escrow?

▶ You accept an offer.

▶ The buyer does their inspections.

▶ You provide the Seller Disclosures. (Facts you know about the property.)

▶ The buyer finalizes financing & appraisal.

▶ Final walk-through. (*Last chance for the buyer to check the home!*)

▶ Closing: You sign all necessary documents to transfer ownership. In some states, funds are disbursed immediately upon signing and in others, you receive payment once escrow processes the funds post-closing.

What Can Delay Closing?

▶ **Buyer Financing Issues:** If their loan falls through, you're back to square one.

- ▸ **Low Appraisal:** If the home appraises below the offer price, negotiations start *again*.
- ▸ **Inspection Surprises:** Major problems = possible re-negotiations.

Pro Tip:

Stay flexible but firm. Closing delays happen, but a good agent will keep things moving forward.

Selling Like a Pro (Without Losing Your Mind)

Selling a home is a rollercoaster, but with the right strategy, it doesn't have to be stressful.

Key Takeaways:

- ▸ **Price your home right.** Overpricing = no offers. Underpricing = leaving money on the table.
- ▸ **Staging sells homes faster.** Clean, declutter, and let in the light!
- ▸ **Negotiate like a pro.** Look at the full offer, not just the price.
- ▸ **Closing can be bumpy.** Stay patient, but stay on top of the details.

Once you hand over the keys and collect your check, you'll feel a mix of relief, excitement, and possibly the urge to buy another house. (In which case, flip back to Chapter 3!)

House it Done?

Selling your home is both an art and a strategy. Do it right, and you'll walk away with a great deal—and maybe even your sanity intact.

Homeownership Horror Stories & Lessons Learned

(Because We All Have Them!)

Let's be real—owning a home is *not* always the picture-perfect dream you see on HGTV. Sure, there are cozy nights by the fireplace and joyful moments of DIY triumph, but there are also plumbing disasters, unexpected expenses, and the occasional rogue animal making itself at home.

Every homeowner has a horror story (or ten), and if they say they don't— they're either lying or haven't owned their home long enough.

In this chapter, we'll share:

- ✓ **Funny, ridiculous, and horrifying tales from real homeowners**
- ✓ **Lessons learned the hard way (so you don't make the same mistakes!)**
- ✓ **Final words of wisdom for surviving the adventure of homeownership**

Buckle up. **This is going to be entertaining.**

Homeownership Horror Stories (That'll Make You Feel Better About Your Life)

The Slow Leak

"I bought my first house and was feeling so proud—didn't move in for about a week after closing day. The weather that week was very humid and warm. Turns out, the kitchen sink pipes had a slow leak that no one uncovered. Went to move in and found mold infesting everything under the kitchen sink and all the walls behind the cabinets. Never knew how fast that could grow. **I learned always to turn off the water temporarily if not going to be at the home on a daily basis."**

Our First Guest

"We bought a house with a lovely backyard. A couple weeks after moving in, we went downstairs and found a large gopher snake on THE KITCHEN FLOOR! We carefully got a shovel and placed it in a bucket and relocated it to the reserve behind the house. I don't even know how it could have gotten in the house but **always ask about unwanted nearby guests.'"**

The "Move-In Ready" Disaster

"We thought we bought a 'move-in ready' home. The whole home had been recently renovated. The home inspector noted that the roof was in 'okay' shape. Within a month, the roof started leaking massively through the bathroom ceiling. How? At least now we could update the bathroom but not without a huge headache. **Moral of the story? Always invest in a roof inspection."**

The Bee Invasion

"I kept witnessing groups of bees around the edge of my roof and figured they just made a hive up near the fascia board on the second story. I would never had assumed they moved right in to the walls. I hired a professional bee

*company to come investigate and they ripped open a hole in the ceiling and wall of the primary room to find a 4'x5' hive the bees had built inside the walls. It took a professional (and a lot of emotional strength) to evict them. Lesson learned: **Always get a full pest/rodent inspection when buying the home to know what you're in for.***"

Lessons from the Trenches: What People Wish They Had Known Before Buying

Now that we've laughed (or cried) over these stories, let's talk about what real homeowners wish they had known **before** buying.

Lesson #1: Inspections Are NOT Optional

If you're tempted to skip a home inspection (*maybe to win a bidding war*), don't do it. That small gamble can turn into a financial nightmare.

- **Get an inspection.** Even if the house looks perfect.
- **If something feels "off," dig deeper.** That "small leak" could be a sign of major plumbing issues.
- **Ask for repair records.** If the sellers can't prove they've maintained the home, assume they haven't.

Lesson #2: The "Oh-Crap" Fund is Mandatory

New homeowners often **underestimate** how much money they'll need for unexpected repairs.

- **Have at least 3-6 months' worth of home expenses saved.**
- **Budget for maintenance**—things will break, and they won't care if you just spent all your savings on closing costs.
- **The first year of homeownership is expensive.** Plan for it.

Lesson #3: DIY Can Be a Slippery Slope

There's nothing wrong with rolling up your sleeves and fixing things yourself—but know your limits.

> ▸ **Painting a room?** Sure.
> ▸ **Installing your own light fixtures?** Maybe.
> ▸ **Rewiring your electrical panel?** Call an electrician unless you like playing with fire—literally.

What Every Homeowner Should Know

Homeownership is a mix of joy, chaos, and life lessons. It's one of the biggest investments you'll ever make—so make sure you go into it with your eyes wide open.

Key Takeaways:

> ▸ **Houses come with surprises.** (And not always good ones.)
> ▸ **Your budget should include repairs & maintenance.**
> ▸ **If something feels "off" during an inspection, investigate.**
> ▸ **Owning a home is an adventure—expect the unexpected.**

At the end of the day, is homeownership worth it?

Absolutely. Despite the horror stories, there's nothing like having a place to call your own.

So, whether you're about to buy your first home, thinking of selling, or already in the trenches of homeownership—know that you're not alone.

And if nothing else, at least you'll have some hilarious stories to tell at dinner parties.

House it Done?

Homeownership is a rollercoaster, but if you go in prepared, you'll handle the challenges like a pro. And one day, when a friend buys their first home, you'll be the one laughing while sharing your own horror stories.

YOU SURVIVED!

(Now, Start Saving for the Next One)

Take a deep breath—**YOU DID IT.** You made it through the wild, unpredictable, and sometimes downright ridiculous journey of homeownership.

Whether you're a brand-new homeowner, a seasoned real estate investor, or someone who just survived selling a house without losing your mind, you now have something invaluable: knowledge.

Owning a home isn't just about having a roof over your head. It's about building wealth, creating stability, and investing in your future. Sure, there were bumps along the way (*like that one unexpected repair that nearly made you cry*), but you navigated them like a pro.

Let's take a moment to recap what you've learned.

What You've Learned on This Adventure

1. **Buying a home isn't just about the mortgage**—you have to be financially prepared for hidden costs, maintenance, and unexpected surprises.
2. **The homebuying process is a rollercoaster, but knowledge is power**—from getting pre-approved to negotiating escrow, you now know how to make smart, strategic moves.

3. **Inspections are your best friend**—even if they reveal terrifying things (*hello, foundation cracks*), knowing what you're getting into saves you money and stress in the long run.

4. **Selling a home is an art**—from staging to pricing, you now understand how to sell like a pro and maximize your profit.

5. **Real estate investing isn't a get-rich-quick scheme, but it builds long-term wealth**—whether you go for a fixer-upper or a turnkey rental, you know how to run the numbers and invest wisely.

6. **Every homeowner has a horror story, but that's part of the fun.** (Bee hives in the attic? Plumbing nightmares? Been there, done that.)

How to Keep Your Home an Asset (Not a Financial Burden)

Owning a home is only a good investment if you take care of it. Letting maintenance slide, overextending yourself financially, or ignoring warning signs can turn your dream home into a money pit.

Simple Ways to Protect Your Investment:

▸ **Follow a maintenance schedule** – Don't wait until things break to fix them.

▸ **Stay on top of home value trends** – Know when it's a good time to refinance or sell.

▸ **Be mindful of home improvements** – Not all upgrades add value (*think twice before adding that neon-green backsplash*).

▸ **Keep an emergency fund** – Because houses have a way of surprising you (*and not in a good way*).

> **Pro Tip:**
>
> A home should be a source of stability, not stress. Make financial decisions that keep you comfortable—not just house-poor.

What's Next? Your Future Real Estate Adventures

Now that you've been through the homeownership gauntlet, what's next?

▸ **Buying a second home?** Maybe a vacation house or an investment property is in your future.

▸ **Renovating?** You now know which upgrades are worth it and which ones aren't.

▸ **Selling?** You're no longer a newbie—you know how to stage, price, and negotiate like a pro.

▸ **Investing?** Maybe you're ready to take the plunge into rental properties or house flipping.

No matter what your next move is, one thing is certain: You've gained the knowledge and confidence to navigate real estate like a boss. Real estate is one of the greatest wealth-building tools out there. It's not always easy, but it's always worth it.

Your home is more than just a place to live—it's an investment in your future.

Your financial decisions today will shape your legacy tomorrow.

You now have the knowledge to make smart, strategic real estate moves.

So whether you're staying put, buying again, or dreaming about your next real estate adventure, just remember: **You've got this!**

Homeownership is a journey—sometimes chaotic, sometimes amazing, but always worth it. Keep learning, keep saving, and keep dreaming big—because who knows? Your next home may be the dream escape you never saw coming!

EXTRAS & WORKSHEETS

- ✓ **Homebuying Budget Worksheet** (Track your income, expenses, and savings goals)
- ✓ **Saving for Your Down Payment** (Put a plan in motion to save money each month for your down payment)
- ✓ **Closing Costs Breakdown** (So you know where your money's going)
- ✓ **Home Maintenance Checklist** (Seasonal and annual upkeep tasks to avoid costly surprises)
- ✓ **Investment Property Readiness Quiz** (Are you really ready to be a landlord?)

The Homebuying Budget Worksheet

(Can You Afford This Adventure?)

This is the part where you get real with your finances. Before jumping into house hunting, fill out this worksheet to see if you're truly ready.

Monthly Income

Take-Home Pay: $_____

Other Monthly Income: $_____

Total Monthly Income: $_____

Monthly Expenses (Before Homeownership)

Rent: $_____

Car Payment & Insurance: $_____

Phone & Internet: $_____

Groceries & Dining Out: $_____

Fun Money: $_____

Credit Card & Other Debt Payments: $_____

Total Monthly Expenses: $_____

Future Homeownership Costs

Estimated Mortgage Payment: $_____

Property Taxes: $_____

Homeowners Insurance: $_____

Utilities & Bills: $_____

Maintenance Fund (1-3% of home value/year): $_____

Total Homeownership Costs: $_____

Savings Check

Current Savings for Down Payment: $_____

Closing Costs Savings: $_____

Emergency Fund: $_____

Final Question: Do you have enough savings AND can you comfortably afford all of the above?

☐ **YES!** Let's do this!

☐ **NO!** Okay, let's make a plan to get there.

Saving for Your Down Payment

Know Your Goal

Estimated Home Price: _____

Down Payment Goal (%): _____

Estimated Closing Costs (3% of home price): _____

Total Savings Goal (Down Payment + Closing Costs): _____

Assess Your Current Savings

Current Savings for Home: _____

Savings Gap (Goal - Current Savings): _____

⏳ Target Date to Reach Goal: _____

Make a Savings Plan

How Much to Save Per Month?

(Savings Gap ÷ Months Until Goal) = _____ per month

Can you realistically save this amount? (Check one)

☐ YES! ☐ Not quite... need adjustments

Step 4: Boost Your Savings

Ways to Save More Each Month (Check off what works for you!)

✓ **Cut Unnecessary Expenses:**

    ☐ Eat out less

    ☐ Cancel unused subscriptions

☐ Reduce gas/transportation costs

☐ Pause non-essential shopping. (Yes, that means Amazon too!)

✓ Increase Your Income:

☐ Take on freelance/gig work

☐ Sell unused items

☐ Consider a side hustle

✓ Automate Your Savings:

☐ Set up automatic transfers to a down payment account

☐ Open a high-yield savings account for better interest

✓ Explore Assistance Programs:

▸ First-time homebuyer grants

▸ Employer homebuyer benefits

▸ Down payment assistance programs

Step 5: Track Your Progress!

Monthly Savings Log

Month	Amount Saved	Hit Monthly Savings Goal	New Savings Total
January		☐	
February		☐	
March		☐	
April		☐	
May		☐	
June		☐	
July		☐	
August		☐	
September		☐	
October		☐	
November		☐	
December		☐	

*Stay consistent, **celebrate small wins**, and watch your home savings grow!*

Homebuying Closing Costs Breakdown

(What You're Really Paying for at Closing)

Closing costs are the final hurdle before you officially own your home. They include various fees and expenses that come with finalizing your mortgage and transferring ownership of the property. Expect to pay 1% to 3% of the home's purchase price in closing costs.

Here's a **detailed breakdown** of where your money is going:

1. Loan-Related Costs

Loan Origination Fee (0.5% – 1% of the loan amount)
▸ This is what your lender charges for processing your mortgage.

Credit Report Fee (*$30 – $50*)
▸ Covers the cost of pulling your credit report for loan approval.

Underwriting Fee (*$500 – $1,200*)
▸ Pays for the lender's evaluation of your financial risk.

Appraisal Fee (*$400 – $800*)
▸ Required by lenders to confirm the home's value before approving the loan.

Discount Points (Optional)
▸ You can **pay extra upfront** to lower your mortgage interest rate.

Lender Title Insurance (about 0.002 of the loan amount)
▸ Protects the mortgage lender—not you—against any potential ownership disputes, title defects, or legal claims on the property.

2. Title & Legal Fees

Title Search Fee (est. *$200 – $500*)

▸ Ensures there are no ownership disputes or outstanding liens on the property.

Title Insurance (est. $1,000 – $3,000, varies by state)

▸ Protects you (and your lender) from title-related legal claims.

Escrow Fee / Closing Fee (est. $1,000 – $2,500, varies by state and purchase price)

▸ Pays for the third party (escrow company or attorney) handling the transaction.

Recording Fee (est. *$150 – $250*)

▸ Charged by your local government to officially record your new home purchase.

Transfer Taxes (if applicable)

▸ A tax some states or counties charge when property ownership is transferred.

Misc. Fees

▸ Notary Fee (est. $150-300)
▸ Wire Fee (est. $50)
▸ Messenger Fee (est. $150)
▸ Loan Tie-In (est. $250)

3. Prepaid Costs (Upfront Housing Expenses)

Homeowners Insurance (1 Year Prepaid) (*$800 – $2,500*)

▸ Most lenders require you to pay your first year of homeowners insurance upfront.

Property Taxes (2-6 Months Prepaid)
- ▸ You may need to prepay a portion of your property taxes to set up your escrow account.

Prepaid Interest
- ▸ Covers interest from your closing date until the first mortgage payment is due.

4. Other Potential Fees ✂

Home Inspection Fee (est. *$400 – $700*)
- ▸ Optional but highly recommended to check the home's condition before buying.
- ▸ A la carte additional inspections may be added on for extra cost and deeper investigations.

Survey or Structural Report (est. *$300 – $800, if applicable*)
- ▸ Some lenders or municipalities require a survey or structural inspection to confirm property characteristics.

HOA Transfer Fee ($300 – $600, if applicable)
- ▸ Covers the cost of transferring ownership in a homeowners association (HOA) community.

How to Lower Closing Costs

Ask the seller to cover closing costs (*Seller concessions are negotiable!*)

Shop around for lenders and title companies (Compare fees before choosing)

Negotiate lender fees (*Some fees can be reduced or waived!*)

📌 **Pro Tip:**

Ask for a Loan Estimate from your lender early in the process. This document breaks down your expected closing costs, so there are no surprises at closing.

Be Financially Prepared!

Closing costs aren't the fun part of buying a home, but they're the price of admission to homeownership. You didn't think snagging the biggest asset of your life would be free, did you? Budgeting ahead of time helps avoid last-minute surprises—so you can stress less and pop the champagne when you get the keys!

Home Maintenance Checklist

(Seasonal & Annual Upkeep Tasks to Avoid Costly Surprises!)

Proper home maintenance keeps your home safe, energy-efficient, and free from expensive repairs. Use this checklist to stay on top of **monthly, seasonal, and annual** tasks so you can prevent problems before they start!

Monthly Home Maintenance

- ✓ **Check & Replace HVAC Filters** (*Every 3-6 months, depending on use*)
- ✓ **Test Smoke & Carbon Monoxide Detectors**
- ✓ **Check for Leaks Under Sinks & Around Toilets**
- ✓ **Inspect HVAC Vents for Dust & Blockages**
- ✓ **Clean Garbage Disposal** (*Use ice cubes, lemon peels, and baking soda*)
- ✓ **Inspect Grout & Caulking in Bathrooms/Kitchen** (*Re-caulk if needed to prevent water damage*)
- ✓ **Flush Toilets & Run Water in Seldom-Used Bathrooms** (*Prevents clogs & dry pipes*)

Spring Home Maintenance (Fresh Start!)

- ☐ **Inspect Roof for Winter Damage** (*Look for missing or damaged shingles!*)
- ☐ **Clean Gutters & Downspouts** (*Prevent water damage & foundation issues*)
- ☐ **Service Air Conditioning Unit** (*Schedule HVAC check-up before summer heat!*)

- ☐ **Check for Cracks in Driveway & Sidewalks** (*Seal them before they get worse!*)
- ☐ **Test & Turn on Sprinkler System**
- ☐ **Wash Windows & Replace Screens if Needed**
- ☐ **Trim Trees & Shrubs Away from House** (*Prevents pest infestations & roof damage*)
- ☐ **Deep Clean Outdoor Furniture & Grill** (*BBQ season is coming!*)

Summer Home Maintenance (Stay Cool & Safe!)

- ☐ **Inspect & Clean Ceiling Fans** (*Switch blades to counterclockwise for cool airflow!*)
- ☐ **Check & Repair Window & Door Seals** (*Keeps cool air in, saves energy!*)
- ☐ **Power Wash Deck, Patio, & Siding** (*Removes dirt, mold, & grime!*)
- ☐ **Check Attic for Signs of Pests or Leaks**
- ☐ **Inspect & Touch Up Exterior Paint** (*Protects against weather damage!*)
- ☐ **Test Sump Pump (If You Have One)**
- ☐ **Clean & Inspect Outdoor Drains & Gutters** (*Summer storms can bring heavy rain!*)

Fall Home Maintenance (Prepare for Cold Weather!)

- ☐ **Clean Gutters & Downspouts Again** (*Prevent ice dams in winter!*)
- ☐ **Service & Inspect Heating System** (*Furnace check-up before it gets cold!*)

- ☐ **Check Chimney & Fireplace** (*Clean before first fire of the season!*)
- ☐ **Seal Cracks Around Windows & Doors** (*Saves heating costs!*)
- ☐ **Drain & Store Garden Hoses** (*Prevents freezing & bursting!*)
- ☐ **Winterize Sprinkler System** (*Shut off water & blow out pipes!*)
- ☐ **Inspect Roof for Loose or Damaged Shingles** (*Snow & ice can make minor issues worse!*)
- ☐ **Stock Up on Winter Essentials** (*Ice melt, snow shovel, emergency kits!*)

Winter Home Maintenance (Cold Weather Survival!)

- ☐ **Check for Ice Dams on Roof** (*Prevents leaks & damage!*)
- ☐ **Test & Maintain Humidifier** (*Prevents dry air & static electricity!*)
- ☐ **Insulate Pipes in Unheated Areas** (*Avoid frozen pipes!*)
- ☐ **Reverse Ceiling Fans to Clockwise Mode** (*Circulates warm air down!*)
- ☐ **Check Basement for Moisture & Leaks**
- ☐ **Keep Walkways & Driveway Clear of Ice & Snow** (*Safety first!*)
- ☐ **Inspect & Clean Dryer Vent** (*Prevents fire hazards!*)

Annual Home Maintenance (The Big Picture Tasks!)

- ☐ **Schedule HVAC Inspection & Tune-Up (Spring & Fall)**
- ☐ **Deep Clean Carpets & Floors**
- ☐ **Inspect Plumbing for Leaks & Corrosion**
- ☐ **Test Garage Door Safety Sensors**
- ☐ **Check Foundation for Cracks or Water Damage**

- ☐ **Inspect Water Heater & Flush Sediment** (*Extends lifespan & efficiency!*)
- ☐ **Check & Clean Exhaust Fans (Kitchen & Bathrooms)**
- ☐ **Service & Inspect Major Appliances** (*Fridge, oven, dishwasher, etc.*)
- ☐ **Trim Trees & Remove Dead Branches** (*Prevents storm damage!*)
- ☐ **Inspect & Clean Septic System (If Applicable)**

Bonus: Home Maintenance Pro Tips!

- ✓ **Set calendar reminders** for seasonal tasks so you never forget!
- ✓ **Keep a home maintenance log**—track repairs, service dates, and costs.
- ✓ **Budget for unexpected repairs**—homeowners should set aside 1-3% of home **value per year** for maintenance.
- ✓ **Fix small issues before they become big ones!** (*A tiny leak today could be a $$$ flood tomorrow!*)

Taking care of your home isn't just about keeping it pretty—it's about protecting your investment. Stay on top of these tasks, and your home will take care of you for years to come!

Investment Property Readiness Quiz

(Are You Really Ready to Be a Landlord?)

Thinking about buying an investment property? Before you dive in, take this quiz to see if you're truly ready for the financial, logistical, and emotional challenges of being a landlord.

Grab a pen and keep track of your answers!

1. Do you have enough savings for a down payment and closing costs?

- ☐ A) Yes, I have at least 15-25% saved for a down payment and extra for closing costs.
- ☐ B) Sort of—I have some money saved, but I might need to stretch my finances.
- ☐ C) Nope, I was hoping to do this with zero down.

Reality Check:

Most lenders require 15-25% down for investment properties, and closing costs can add 2-5% of the purchase price.

2. Do you have a financial cushion for unexpected repairs and vacancies?

- ☐ A) Yes, I have 3-6 months' worth of expenses saved up for emergencies.
- ☐ B) I have some savings, but I'd be in trouble if a major repair came up.
- ☐ C) No, I was planning to use my rental income to cover everything.

Reality Check:

Rental income isn't always consistent—vacancies, late payments, and emergency repairs happen. A financial cushion is essential.

3. Have you calculated your potential cash flow?

- ☐ A) Yes! I've run the numbers and my rental income will cover my expenses with profit left over.
- ☐ B) I've estimated some numbers, but I'm not 100% sure if it's profitable.
- ☐ C) No, I just assume rent will cover the mortgage and I'll be fine.

Reality Check:

Successful landlords know their numbers. Factor in mortgage, insurance, property taxes, maintenance, and vacancies before assuming you'll make money.

4. How do you feel about dealing with tenants?

- ☐ A) No problem! I'm ready for tenant screenings, lease agreements, and maintenance calls.
- ☐ B) I'd rather not, but I'd consider hiring a property manager.
- ☐ C) Absolutely not—I just want to collect rent and never hear from anyone.

Reality Check:

Being a landlord isn't passive. If you don't want to deal with tenants, budget for a property manager (8-12% of monthly rent).

5. Are you prepared for the legal responsibilities of being a landlord?

☐ A) Yes, I've researched local landlord-tenant laws and fair housing rules.

☐ B) I know a little, but I need to learn more.

☐ C) Wait... there are laws?

Reality Check:

Landlord-tenant laws vary by state and can include eviction rules, security deposit limits, and maintenance obligations. Ignorance isn't an excuse!

6. Have you decided on a fixer-upper or a turnkey rental?

☐ A) I have a plan—I know what I want and what I can handle.

☐ B) I'm unsure, but I'm open to both.

☐ C) I'll buy whatever looks cheap.

Reality Check:

Fixer-uppers can be great investments, but renovations cost time and money. Turnkey rentals are easier but may have smaller profit margins.

7. Are you prepared for property management?

☐ A) Yes, I can handle tenant screening, rent collection, and maintenance.

☐ B) I'd rather hire a property manager, but I understand the costs.

☐ C) No, I just assumed renters would take care of everything themselves.

> **Reality Check:**
>
> Even with a property manager, you're still responsible for keeping your property profitable and legal.

8. How long are you willing to hold the property?

☐ A) At least 5+ years—I know real estate is a long-term game.
☐ B) 2-5 years—I might sell it if the market is good.
☐ C) I just want to flip it quickly for a profit.

> **Reality Check:**
>
> Real estate investing is a long-term strategy. Quick flips require market expertise and can be risky.

9. What's your backup plan if the property doesn't generate profit immediately?

☐ A) I have multiple income streams and a financial cushion.
☐ B) I'd be okay for a little while but would feel the pressure.
☐ C) I'm relying 100% on the rental income to cover my mortgage.

> **Reality Check:**
>
> A bad tenant, market downturn, or unexpected repair can hurt your profits. Always have a Plan B.

10. Why do you want to invest in real estate?

☐ A) I want to build long-term wealth and financial security.
☐ B) I want passive income (but I know it's not *truly* passive).
☐ C) I just heard it's a good way to get rich quick.

Reality Check:

Real estate is not a get-rich-quick scheme. It's a wealth-building tool that requires patience, strategy, and planning.

Your Investment Readiness Results

Mostly A's: You're Ready!

You've done your research, planned for expenses, and understand what it takes to be a landlord. You're prepared to buy and manage an investment property like a pro. Go forth and start building your real estate empire!

Mostly B's: You're Getting There!

You're on the right track but still have some financial and knowledge gaps to fill. Before you buy, work on increasing savings, running the numbers, and researching landlord responsibilities.

Mostly C's: Hold Up!

You might not be fully prepared for the realities of real estate investing yet. Do more research, build a financial cushion, and learn about property management before jumping in. Real estate can be profitable—but only if you go in with a solid plan.

Owning an investment property can be a great way to build wealth—but it's not for everyone. The key is preparation.

If your quiz results say you're ready, go for it! If you're not quite there yet, don't rush—keep learning, saving, and preparing.

When the right opportunity comes along, you'll be ready to invest with confidence!